# BREWED AWAKENINGS

"O coffee!
Thou dost dispel all care,
Thou art the object of desire to the scholar.
This is the beverage of the friends of god."

—Arabic poem "In Praise of Coffee"

An Illustrated Journey to
Coffeehouses in Wisconsin
...and Beyond*

*That is, around the Rim and into Duluth, Minneapolis, St. Paul,
and McGregor, Iowa, as chosen by the
intrepid and a bit jittery artist and author,

# JEFF HAGEN

First edition, first printing
Copyright © 2007 Jeff Hagen

Design: Flying Fish Graphics, Blue Mounds, WI
Printed in Canada

Library of Congress Cataloging-in-Publication Data

Hagen, Jeff.
  Brewed awakenings : an illustrated journey to coffeehouses in Wisconsin and beyond / Jeff Hagen. — 1st ed.
     p. cm.
  ISBN-13: 978-0-9761450-9-7 (alk. paper)
  1. Coffeehouses—Wisconsin—Guidebooks. 2. Coffeehouses—Minnesota—Guidebooks. 3. Coffeehouses—
Iowa—Guidebooks. I. Title.
  TX907.3.W6H34 2007
  647.9509775—dc22

                    2007031047

Itchy Cat Press
an Imprint of Flying Fish Graphics
5452 Highway K
Blue Mounds, Wisconsin 53517
ffg@mhtc.net

In loving memory of Grace Eleanor Bakke-Hagen
"Mom"

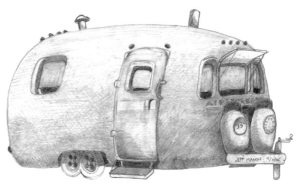

## About the Author

Jeff Hagen is a best-selling author and artist of seven published books, including two award winners: *Steeple Chase* and *Hiawatha Passing*. The latter was acclaimed by numerous critics, including the *Milwaukee Journal, Publishers Weekly, Kirkus Reviews*, N.E.A., the Junior Library Guild of America, and the *New York Times*, which honored it as one of the 10 best children's books in America (1995).

Jeff also writes and illustrates cover stories and travel features for many regional and national newspapers, including the *Chicago Tribune, St. Paul Pioneer Press, Sunday Detroit News, Minneapolis Star Tribune, Wisconsin State Journal, The Capital Times*, and *Milwaukee Journal Sentinel*. His stories and artwork have appeared in *Wisconsin Trails, Cricket*, and *Outside* magazines. Internationally, his work appeared in the *Beijing Review* in the People's Republic of China.

Jeff's artworks have appeared in juried shows and exhibitions across the U.S. and Europe. His books have been featured on TV's Food Channel and "Good Morning America".

Visit his website: jeffhagenart.com.

"As soon as coffee is in your stomach, there is a general commotion,
ideas begin to move.... Similes arise, the paper is covered.
Coffee is your ally and writing ceases to be a struggle."

—Honoré de Balzac

# CONTENTS

# BEYOND THE RIM

"It was a pleasant café, warm and clean and friendly, and I hung up my old water-proof on the coat rack to dry and put my worn and weathered felt hat on the rack above the bench and ordered a café au lait. The waiter brought it and I took out a notebook from the pocket of the coat and a pencil and started to write."

—Ernest Hemingway

In a remote corner of Iowa, flying saucer
sightings are daily occurrences.
Stanton Water Tower, Stanton, Iowa

# FROM ETHIOPIA TO EAGLE RIVER
## A Short History of Coffee

Legend has it that coffee was discovered NOT by the Hills Brothers, Juan Valdez, or Mrs. Olson.

No, coffee was discovered by animals.

### The Story of Kalidi and his Amazing Goats

The tale is told that over a thousand years ago there once was a young goat herder in Ethiopia, named Kalidi.

Kalidi was a poet and musician.

Every day he would lead his goats up paths that led out of his small village and up the mountain that loomed above the boy's valley. He would sit down on a comfortable rock and let the goats disperse and forage up the mountain.

When the sun began to dip low in the sky, Kalidi would blow a sharp note on his flute. Hearing this, the goats would scamper down the mountainside and gather around Kalidi.

Well, one day, Kalidi blew on his flute. No goats!

He blew again. None appeared!

So he began to search for his missing herd.

By and by, he came upon a clearing, high up the mountain, where he found his goats.

They were acting very strange.

They were jumping and butting each other and running around in a frisky manner. Shocked, Kalidi was convinced that they had become demonically possessed!

Curiosity got the better of him and he stopped to observe what was causing the erratic behavior. He noticed that some of the goats were chewing on berries from the surrounding bushes.

He picked some and chewed them. Soon, he became light-headed and euphoric. He gathered his herd and took a handful of the "magic berries" down to the village where he encountered the local imam. Whereupon he told the story of the goats and gave the berries to the imam.

The imam took the berries and experimented with them. He dried them and boiled them in water to produce a hot drink. He used the drink to keep himself alert and awake during religious ceremonies.

Word spread about the magic berries and the unusual effect that they had on one's condition and attitude. Soon the whole village climbed up the mountain, gathered the berries, bagged them, and returned to their homes to indulge in and savor the new buzz about town.

With a little imagination, they tried steaming the berries, and later named them "beans" and served them as a drink. The town became known as the coffee merchant village and of course, as they say, the rest is history.

Thanks a Latte, Goat Boy!

Well, it's a good story that pops up in coffee history books and on the internet. (An observant coffee drinker might notice how many brands of coffee in America use the name Kalidi in various brews and brands of coffee.)

Case in point:

As I wrote this, I sat in a coffeehouse in West Lafayette, Indiana.

I asked them what coffee brand they have at the counter. "Dancing Goats" was the answer.

Small world, isn't it?

Yes, small world indeed. And it's coffee-flavored.

## Follow the Bean

Geographically and historically, it is a long trek from Ethiopia to Eagle River.

Let's pick up the historic trail marker at the 1950 entrance ramp when coffee shops began to take root in Contemporary American Culture.

Coffee in the 1950s was dominated by the large store-bought brands, including Maxwell House, Hills Brothers, Folger's, and others.

Big cans with little taste.

In fact, blandness was almost the common denominator of American coffee back then.

No surprise that here was a great need for good coffee.

A need that took root and manifested itself in the form of esoteric coffeehouses in the large cities of New York and San Francisco. Especially San Francisco.

In 1957, Giovanni Grotto, a local window washer, opened The Café Trieste in the North Beach section of San Francisco.

ADDIS ABABA

SIX FLAGS OVER ZAMBIA

EAGLE RIVER

More than a purveyor of Italian-style and espresso coffee, the café soon became a gathering spot for beat poets like Allen Ginsberg and Jack Kerouac.

It was here, in North Beach, that the late newspaper columnist Herb Caen coined the word "beatnik" to describe the group of poets and culturists who frequented Café Trieste.

San Francisco also was a port city. The city's harbor gave small coffee entrepreneurs the advantage of selling high-quality coffee right off the ships arriving from South America.

One notable coffee house pioneer was Alfred Peet.

Peet was determined to bring good quality coffee to the public. With a modest inheritance from his father, along with a used twenty-five-pound coffee roaster and ten bags of Colombian coffee beans, he opened Peet's Coffee & Tea in Berkeley (1966).

His shop was small and modest with a coffee bar that offered six stools for patrons to sit and sip. Word spread that this was a unique and delightful coffee experience. The coffee was stronger than the typically weak commercial brands at the supermarket.

Within a year, the line of people trying to get into Peet's stretched around the block.

Peet's flourished and word quickly got around that this was a place of quality in a small storefront setting without pretense or commercial fuss.

Like a new tree, the idea of coffeehouses took root and spread across the land. A new aroma permeated the American cultural landscape: the scent of fresh roasted coffee that drifted out of revitalized storefront shops across America.

It had the unmistakable smell of success.

Up the West Coast from San Francisco, another port city picked up the scene.

### Fill it to the Brim on the Pacific Rim

In Seattle, three enterprising college students refurbished an old storefront shop (where the rent was $137 a month) and created the original Starbucks.

The original owners sold the business to an entrepreneur who enlarged and franchised Starbucks into the giant international chain that it is today.

Starbucks has become the Goliath of coffee shops across the country.

But for every Goliath, there must of course be a David.

### Here comes Eagle River.

The true embodiment of David can be found in the collection of small coffeehouses throughout our country.

One-of-a-kind coffeehouses, they slowly spread from the West Coast to the Midwest. At first, they took root in midwestern cities, followed by college towns and tourist locations, like Eagle River.

Nowadays, one can find good coffee shops in the tiniest of villages and burgs. Take for instance, Rochester, Wisconsin (population 1,100), which has a wonderful coffee emporium called Stir Crazy.

In larger towns, they have created their own renaissance.

A rebirth of Main Street.

In Platteville, Bob Metzger of Badger Brothers Coffee café defined the Main Street renaissance this way.

"In the old days, Main Street America was a place where everyone came to buy shoes, overalls, dry goods and a place where they could trade eggs and produce. They also came to Main Street to get caught up on the nourishment of community news and recent doings around town."

Then came the era of urban sprawl, suburbia, big box discount stores, and malling of America. Main Street faded and folded in the face of the changing winds of commerce.

Today we have a few independent visionaries who have bought old vintage buildings on Main Street.

They have opened coffee shops and brought back the heartbeat of Main Street once again.

Places that harken back to the old independent philosophy of good products, trustworthy service, and strong individual character.

Good coffeehouses serve up this trait like bottomless pots of coffee.

Perhaps their most important commodity is the fact that these small businesses provide a place where people can linger and talk to each other. The stock and trade of the human heart.

A community watering hole—the center of the Universe down on Main Street.

•

"He was my cream and I was his coffee and when you poured us together, it was something."

—Josephine Baker

Ashland
# THE BLACK CAT COFFEEHOUSE
211 Chapple Avenue

"I purchased the old downtown building that formerly was The Black Cat Saloon.

"I had the lofty dream of opening my own business. I wanted to create a community gathering place with a different mission and purpose than a saloon.

"I decided that this building's new life would be that of a coffeehouse.

"Originally, before the building was a bar, it was a butcher shop with a back room for meat storage.

"Today that room has a totally new and different life—it is our vegetarian kitchen!

"One of my favorite stories about 'coffee moments' at The Black Cat is when one of my regular customer reminisced about the times that she had to come down here and drag her husband out of the saloon after he'd spent hours of imbibing.

"Ironically nowadays, the table has turned and it is she who has to be 'fetched' after having her second latte of the day."

— Honore Spickerman, owner

Bayfield
# BURT & FRANCIE'S CAFÉ
117 Rittenhouse Avenue

"Burt & Francie's in Bayfield is a great local gathering spot that features a quaint and comfortable atmosphere.

"It's located on Bayfield's Rittenhouse Avenue, the main thoroughfare in this small harbor village on Lake Superior.

"The coffeehouse features baked goods made daily in-house.

"Burt & Francie's offers a limited breakfast and lunch menu with great vegetarian options. All coffees and most of the food products are organic and/or purchased locally."

— Lisa Marshall

•

"Coffee is a fleeting moment and a fragrance."

— Claudia Roden

23

Burlington
# THE DAILY BREW
557 Milwaukee Avenue

"I'm French, and finding a good coffee place in the USA is close to impossible. But, I found one, in my own little town of Burlington, Wisconsin. The Daily Brew—I get my double espresso there every day and once in a while, I'll have a quiche (after all, I am FRENCH).

"It's one of those places where you feel at home.

"The owners, Pat and Kris Clark, are wonderful people. They do a lot for the community and they offer their walls to the artists of Burlington.

"I am so HAPPY that I found this place!"

— Aude Nyhlen, très satisfied customer

25

26

Cornucopia

# SISKIWIT BAY COFFEE & CURIOSITIES

88610 Superior Avenue

We travel north to the northernmost town in Wisconsin.

To Cornucopia, which also has the shortest main street that I've seen in the state, Superior Avenue.

Two blocks long, it has three storefront businesses in its brief commercial exposure. And one of them is a coffee shop.

A very good coffee shop.

Siskiwit Bay Coffee & Curiosities opened a few years ago and frankly, this shop impresses me as one of the best of the 125 shops that I visited in three years of traveling the state sipping coffee.

As an artist and architecture buff, the first impression that I had of this shop was of aesthetic arrest. It is a wonderful send-up of vernacular architecture, blending the old and the new.

Owners Dennis and Barbara Edwards constructed the building to reflect the architectural heritage of the town—a fishing village.

For years, Cornucopia had been a thriving fishing harbor, dotted with small, humble fish houses.

Built of tin and white pine, the fishing houses are as much a part of our state's architectural legacy as the log cabin and wooden farmhouse.

The Edwards incorporated that integrity into the design of their coffee-house.

Architectural wonder, yes, but how 'bout the coffee?

For that answer, let's listen to one of the shop's regular drinkers speak of its inner wonders:

"This is one of the best-kept secrets in a town that is one of Wisconsin's best-kept secrets. Not only is the gourmet coffee outstanding, but the fresh-baked fruit scones each morning are worth getting out of bed for, and the whipping cream melts on the still-warm bread pudding."

— Philip E. Pruss, scone slave

•

"Coffee has two virtues, it is wet and warm."

— Dutch proverb

"The coffee is so strong , you could float a pistol in it."

—Old southern folk saying

•

"I can envision a small cottage somewhere,
With a lot of writing paper, and a dog, and a fireplace
And maybe enough money to give myself some Irish coffee
Now and then and entertain my two friends."

— Lt. Richard Van der Geer

De Pere
# LUNA COFFEE ROASTERS
330 Main Avenue

What is the magic found in this little storefront coffeehouse?

Well, start with this.

Look beyond the menu and take in the ambiance:

A beautiful old storefront, the smell of fresh roasted coffee, soft chatter and laughter, a palpable sense of community.

Look around at the interior and savor the patina of time displayed on the old brick walls.

Great coffee in a vintage building.

The place has a simple name—Luna—and it is a place built on the values of hard work and passion for serving people in a comfortable, inviting environment.

A small business with emphasis on quality and personal service.

Stir it all in.

Sip slowly and enjoy.

There's now a satellite Luna in Door County's Fish Creek.

Author's official coffee vehicle for the trip, "Pony Espresso".

Eagle River
# TERRA NICOLE'S
711 D Highway 45 North

"My favorite beverage at Terra Nicole's is the White Chocolate Iced Mocha which I have treated myself to on a daily basis over the years.

"I've tried to match this mocha on my travels in many states but others have never come close to my expectations. Terra Nicole's has a wide variety of excellent drinks, coffees, pastries, candies, and great breakfasts and lunches."

— Holly Jahnz, customer with taste

Ephraim

# LEROY'S COFFEE SHOP

9922 Water Street

Several years ago, I had the pleasure of interviewing Allen Pape, one of the log home experts at Old World Wisconsin.

Allen would save vintage log structures by buying the old buildings from farmers across Wisconsin.

He would carefully number each log, take the structure apart, and ship the building down to Old World Wisconsin where it would be reconstructed and displayed as a living example of our state's history and heritage.

I was interviewing Allen for a magazine article on log buildings.

It was late in the afternoon. The sun was setting, casting amber rays across the old silver logs.

Allen said, "Look at how the sunrays bring out the ax marks on the logs. That is the signature of labor and toil from log builders a century ago, talking to us over time; it is the literature of the logs."

Well, I saw that literature of the logs and time when I entered Leroy's Coffee Shop on the peninsula of Door County. This is an old vintage building from bygone days of early Wisconsin.

It has all the intrinsic elements that Allen spoke of—and the spirit of the logs.

Today, it has another element, the sweet aroma of coffee brewing.

The fragrance emanates from the building and lingers on main street, ushering in a new morning and a new day in Wisconsin.

Evansville

# REAL COFFEE

18 East Main Street

Real Coffee brings color, culture, and the best Sunday brunch around to this small south central town.

For decades, this Main Street building served another purpose. It was the town's post office. During the week, the locals would gather here, in such frequency that there is a worn path in the wood floor where people stood in line to get their mail and catch up on the talk of the town.

Today, it's still a gathering place, but now the locals are sitting down to enjoy great coffee and eats instead of sanding a path in the floor.

Owners Susan Finque and Maria Martinez moved here from America's coffee capital, Seattle. They soon realized that the nearest genuine coffeehouse was twenty miles away.

So they decided to open their own shop.

In the process they created a new gathering place with a new Main Street mission—a coffee shop featuring a full espresso bar, healthy food, and an environment filled with wonderful local artwork.

Judging from the happy crowd that was in attendance on the morning that I visited, it appears that Real Coffee has won the town's stamp of approval.

Hayward

# BACKROADS COFFEE & TEA

10546 Dakota Avenue


Backroads Coffee enterprise began in 1989 as a mail order business, roasting and shipping coffee all over the United States.

Considered to be "ahead of its time" 18 years ago, the enterprise has evolved into a great coffee shop for the Hayward area.

Today, the coffee shop is located in a beautiful old blacksmith shop (right next to The Moccasin Bar, a classic Northwoods tavern adorned with stuffed animals playing cards). If that's not NORTHERN enough for you, walk a few blocks farther and take in the National Fresh Water Fishing Hall of Fame and Museum, featuring a huge walk-through Musky that looks like a DC–9 on a stick.

Hayward is a trip!

A trip worth taking—and the best place in town to sit down and reflect on its many roadside attractions is at this little brick coffeehouse.

Hurley

# HURLEY COFFEE COMPANY

122 Silver Street


Located on what the locals call "the busiest corner in Northern Wisconsin", Hurley Coffee Company provides more than coffee to its clientele.

This is what one regular penned about HCC:

"Sexy management, beautiful staff, and terrific coffee and teas.
"The place has an ambiance you can't find in Madison or New York City.
"Hurley Coffee Company offers up poetry readings, art displays, tasty menus, and the nicest people in the Northland. No one who has stopped here to have a cup of Joe goes away without a positive experience."

— C. Castagna, happy Hurley customer

Kenosha
# COMMON GROUNDS
5159 Sixth Avenue


"I love this place!

"Actually, this isn't a place,

"It is my oasis.

"It's where I go when I'm thirsty for a hug or when I'm hungry for the need to connect.

"IT ISN'T JUST THE COFFEE,

"It's the welcoming warmth of the people who serve it."

— Sandra Hujik, uncommonly contented customer

"Coffee tastes better with a friend."

—Author unknown

La Crosse

# JULES' COFFEE HOUSE

327 Pearl Street

"One of my favorite coffee places in the entire state is Jules'.

"Whenever I travel to La Crosse, I make a point of stopping at Jules'. They have wonderful scones! There is a neat little bookstore next door and a really eclectic bar down the street called The Casino which actually has an old neon sign from the '40s that says 'Lousy Service'!

"It's great to sit outside at a sidewalk table sipping coffee and taking in the scenery of downtown La Crosse."

— Jane from Lazy Jane's Café in Madison

•

"I have tried to show the café as a place where one can go mad."

— Vincent Van Gogh

GUND
ARENZ SHOES
JULES COFFEE
FRESH COFFEE
OPEN
ESPRESSO
LATTE

LAKE MENDOTA

STATE STREET

JEFF HADEN

BASCOM HILL

## Madison

Our trek through Madison's coffee land begins on one of Wisconsin's most famous streets:

State Street.

State Street is the embodiment of all Main Streets in Wisconsin.

It is the ground zero of culture and entertainment in Dairyland.

Over the years, it has provided an environment ranging from parades to state tournament celebrations. It has seen its share of lawlessness, riots, and demonstrations. Life and death.

Commercially, its mercantile frontage has displayed a variety of offerings: unique boutiques, rowdy bars, fancy eateries, and creative shops and galleries.

Today, State Street has another great feature to offer up:

Coffee shops.

Coffee emporiums so abundant that in one eight-block section of the street there are seven coffee shops.

One might say that State Street is a place that is well grounded.

## **FAIR TRADE COFFEEHOUSE** 418 State Street
## **MICHELANGELO'S COFFEE HOUSE** 114 State Street

Two State Street coffee shop owners, Sam Chehade and Lori Henn, present a perspective on coffee culture beyond the local parameters of State Street, out to the far reaches of the world.

"We truly believe that we are making a difference globally. By carrying fair

trade and organically grown coffees at Michelangelo's and Fair Trade Coffeehouse, everybody wins. The farmers in developing countries receive a fair price, the environment gets a reprieve from pesticides and clear-cutting, and the consumer gets a high-quality product. And as business people we feel a certain pride in participating in this type of global enterprise. For us, this is the only way. We understand the plight of the small farmers as we see it everyday in the Midwest. Perhaps

this trend of considering global and local impact on farmers, as well as on the earth itself, is the wave of the future. We have to think of the sustainability and environmental impact on everything we do."

— Lori Henn and Sam Chehade

Madison
# STEEP AND BREW
544 State Street


Mark Ballering has owned and operated a coffee shop on State Street for 25 years.

Mark opened the first viable coffee shop on State Street, way back in 1979.


So how was it back in the beginning?

"In 1984, we decided to extend our hours to include nights.

"Well, it was so new and different to the State Street culture, that hardly anyone would come in the shop on Friday night.

"One night my wife and I sat up front at a table by the window, just to show people passing by that there were indeed 'signs of life' in here.

"Over time, people started to frequent our shop; mostly it was the foreign students that came in, who really knew about coffee shops from their home countries.

"One day, I was carrying some dishes from the back to the front of the shop. Every table was packed with people. As I passed each table I realized that NO ONE was speaking English, it was all foreign languages."

Today this is one of the most popular coffee shops in town, a fact that speaks volumes in a city that offers over sixty coffee shops.

"If I asked for a cup of coffee, someone would search for the double meaning."

—Mae West

Madison

# CARGO COFFEE

1309 South Park Street

One of the frequent observations that I made on my coffee journey throughout the Midwest, was the fact that many of these popular little java joints are located in older buildings that originally served a different mercantile mission.

This little shop on Madison's south side originally functioned as a Jiffy Lube. Five years ago, owner Lindsey Lee bought the building and gave it a new life.

Cargo Coffee has a strategic location for coffee drinkers who commute into the city. The shop is located on one of the main arteries leading into the campus of the University of Wisconsin. Students, professors, and UW staffers stop on their way to and from campus.

The shop is a great environment for a "third place" to linger between home and the office.

Comfortable digs for weary commuters after a hard day's work in Mad City.

Madison
# LAZY JANE'S CAFÉ
1358 Williamson Street

"Entering Lazy Jane's Café on Madison's quirky Williamson Street is like going back home, if home is warm and cozy and friendly. The furniture here is mismatched, most of it rescued from secondhand shops. The art on the walls is contributed by local artists, and there are artistic 'Janie' touches throughout the old two-story house.

"The bakery counter holds scrumptious cinnamon buns, muffins, and moist flaky scones ('I am the Queen of Scones,' says Janie, with just a touch of pride).

"The menu chalkboard offers hearty breakfasts, soups, salads, and sandwiches. And of course there is a good selection of coffees and teas.

"And then there is Jane herself, warm, loving and outgoing, she is a perfect embodiment of her own café. Any morning or noon will find Lazy Jane's filled with couples, singles, working moms with kids, professionals, and students. For many regulars, Lazy Jane's is truly a home away from home."

—Jerry Minnich, gourmand (and Lazy Jane's frequenter)

LAZY JANE'S CAFE

OPEN

LAZY JANES CAFE

(This is the former Legacy Chocolates building. Don't panic; it just moved down the street.)

Save the Earth. It's the only planet with chocolate!

## Menomonie
# LEGACY CHOCOLATES
643 South Broadway Avenue

Recently, I was invited to be on several talk shows on the public radio network to talk about this coffee book.

The program's host asked me if I needed suggestions from listeners.

When I indicated, yes, I was open for tips and leads, the switchboard lit up brighter than O'Hare airport on a Sunday night.

I jotted down over sixty-five suggested hot spots, in and out of the state of Wisconsin.

One of the places that kept coming up over and over again was a place called Legacy Chocolates.

"Yeah, but, this is a book about coffee, not chocolate," I emphatically stated to those listeners.

"Well, this place also has wonderful coffee," was the reply.

Curiosity got the better of me and I made the long journey to Menomonie to try the coffee.

The tip line was right—the coffee and the chocolate was a double treasure.

Coffee? Chocolate? Why, SURE! Who needs sleep, anyway?

Milwaukee
# ALTERRA AT THE LAKE
1701 North Lincoln Memorial Drive

Located in the historic Milwaukee River Flushing Station, Alterra at the Lake opened in September 2002 and quickly became a popular destination on Milwaukee's lakefront.

The café is operated by Alterra Coffee Roasters, a Wisconsin-based roaster and wholesaler of specialty coffees from Latin America, East Africa, and Southeast Asia.

In my travels across the state, I found a great reverence and respect for this company. (Many of the small roasters obtain their own coffee specialties from Alterra, and the praise for the quality of Alterra's coffee and service was outstanding.)

Alterra has several locations throughout Cream City, but this one stands out for its unique features and location.

The building was constructed in 1888 to house a water pump that at the time was the largest of its kind in the world. In the renovation of the facility, recycled materials and "green" buildings techniques were incorporated wherever possible.

"In Cream City, it's the cat's meow."

The café serves espresso-based beverages and other drinks, baked goods, hot and cold sandwiches, soups and salads, all of which are made daily by Alterra Baking Company.

Milwaukee
# ROCHAMBO COFFEE & TEA HOUSE
1317 East Brady Street

I must admit, I am a sucker for this street and neighborhood on Milwaukee's east side.

I've always viewed the Brady Street neighborhood as a "town within a city".

It has that homey feeling about it.

The shops, bars, and eateries that line Brady Street all have that eclectic sense of individual ma and pa shop owner ambiance.

One-of-a-kind shops.

Of course, Rochambo fits that image.

An old house with an abundant offering of coffee and tea.

A place to step away from the madding crowd; park yourself by the window, plop your feet up, and watch the flow of humanity skate by on a snowy sidewalk.

A homecoming for the soul.

61

Rolls & Trolls

Mount Horeb
# SJÖLINDS CHOCOLATE HOUSE
219 East Main Street


The town of Mount Horeb has a Scandinavian tradition centered on the legendary trolls of Norwegian folklore.

The troll has become Mount Horeb's official icon.

Running through the town is a tree-lined bike trail aptly called the Troll Way. For years a local wood sculptor named Mike Feeney carved large-sized trolls which appeared on street corners and byways throughout the town.

He built a delightful little edifice on Main Street to create his wooden trolls. Nowadays, that former art studio has morphed into a charming little coffee shop.

Owned by Chris and Tracy Thompson, the shop offers up wonderful coffee and fresh pastries. The most popular is Sjölinds' fresh baked truffle cakes.

On the day that I sat and sipped coffee here, I noticed that Sjölinds is a popular place for families with little kids.

It struck me as fitting.

For here is a warm place with a family atmosphere that seems to work, small kids making joyful sounds in a house originally made for tiny folks of legendary stature.

Platteville
# BADGER BROTHERS COFFEE
10 East Main Street

O.K. this is a story about the entrepreneurial spirit of coffee shop owners in Dairyland.

From my perspective, Bob and Linda Metzger represent that intrinsic attitude of "can do" displayed by all of these coffee shops featured within these pages.

Herein lies the tale:

Bob was a successful (well-paid) petroleum engineer in Alaska. He and his talented wife, Linda, looked at their future and decided that there had to be more in life.

They thought about all of this . . . over coffee.

This thought process and planning stage occurred at one of the many coffee houses in Anchorage.

So, in a Eureka! moment, they looked at each other and said "What about this?"

A coffee shop!

Their first step was to ask their favorite coffee shop owner if he would give them advice about how to start.

Bob offered to work for the man in his shop for free in exchange for learning how to be a roaster and barristo.

The owner said, "All right, I'll teach you the stock and trade, but, I insist on paying you for working in the shop."

Bob said, "O.K, if you insist on paying me then make my paycheck out to Habitat for Humanity and donate it every pay period."

Which he did.

After a year, Bob and Linda decided to move back to the Midwest and open their shop, bringing along that experience and bringing along that spirit of "can do".

Which they did.

They picked a little college town, Platteville, and opened Badger Brothers.

And created yet another mercantile renaissance on a main street in Wisconsin.

Prairie du Sac
# BLUE SPOON CAFÉ
550 Water Street

When I first saw this riverside terrace café on a bluff above the Wisconsin River, I thought, "This place reminds me of Italy."

The outside dining area behind the building has a landscape and aesthetic reminiscent of places where I've lingered in Tuscany.

The Blue Spoon Café is a coffee/deli/restaurant created by Craig and Lea Culver, co-founders of Culver's Restaurants, and is located next to Culver's headquarters on Prairie du Sac's main street.

The interior has a beautiful ambiance to it. Stone tiles, handpainted faux plaster walls, mahogany and maple cabinets, and table tops of dark granite. Wrapped inside the elegant interior is a collection of tables filled with happy people.

I asked Mike Boss, director of operations and development, if he had any unique "coffee moments" that stood out in his recollection.

"Well, there is one special story that stands out in my mind. We had a ninety-year-old guest who loved coming in here on a regular basis. When her family asked her what she wanted for her upcoming birthday she had a special request.

'I would love a year's worth of free mochaccinos at the Blue Spoon.'

"The family asked if that was possible from the restaurant's standpoint.

"Well, it was a unique situation. Both the family and the Blue Spoon granted her ninetieth birthday wish."

Racine
# MILAEGER'S JAVA GARDEN CAFÉ

4838 Douglas Avenue

A funny thing happened when I was traveling through Racine last year.

I was looking for one particular coffee shop in town that one of my tipsters from public radio had told me about.

But word got out that I was looking for the best coffee shop in the county and I received a call from a popular local newspaper columnist who asked if I "would be open to more suggestions from the public".

Why not? So, I said yes, and he put the story of my coffee journey and quest in his weekly column, and asked readers to send their suggestions to my e-mail address.

Well, ten days and over 200 e-mails later, I had a pretty extensive idea of the best coffeehouses in this part of Wisconsin! A fact that compelled me to go back to Racine and vicinity numerous times to sample the fare.

Milaeger's was one of the places that I received a ton of mail about.

It is a unique place that started as a garden center in the early 60's.

Now, Milaeger's is the largest grower in the area. The Milaeger family added a café as a convenience for their customers.

Java Garden Café opened and soon became a big hit serving great breakfasts, lunch, desserts, major league Bloody Marys, and of course, excellent coffee.

Their signature coffee is a customized blend from Alterra called Dragonwing, named after a beautiful flower in their greenhouse.

This is a great place to spend time relaxing over a cup of coffee with friends resting alongside an emerald green garden of earthly delights.

•

"The morning cup of coffee has exhilaration about it
which the cheering influence of the afternoon
or evening cup of tea cannot expect to reproduce."

—Oliver Wendell Holmes Sr.

Racine
# MOCHA LISA
2825 4 1/2 Mile Road

Mocha Lisa coffeehouse is literally a house.

Built in 1903, the farmhouse was completely gutted and renovated to create individual rooms that are brightly painted. Walls display painted silks, photography, original oils, acrylics, and watercolors.

It is strikingly obvious that the owners have a strong art background.

There are several rooms, all adorned with artwork and bright colors.

One of the rooms has big comfy chairs and a couch to lounge on.

Mocha Lisa is a coffeehouse filled to the brim with character, warmth, and local color.

"Mocha Lisa is indeed unique to Racine. A nice non-franchise place to have business lunches, meetings, or just solo coffee-sipping time.

"In the summer there is a wonderful garden adjacent to the house to walk out to and enjoy. Mocha Lisa's staff is laid back and friendly, ultimately concerned that your order is just the way you like it."

—Donna Haman, Mocha Lisa regular

Racine
# THE GROUNDS KEEPER
327 Main Street

The Grounds Keeper is tucked away in downtown Racine, one block west of the marina on Lake Michigan. Established in 1996, it was voted "the coziest coffee shop" by Racine's denizens.

This coffeehouse is known for its tasty coffee and fancy espressos, as well as the wide range of deli sandwiches. Save room for dessert—they make gelato ice cream daily right on the premises.

Dedicated customers include judges, scientists, business folks, boaters, students, and regular coffee klatschers.

During the 2004 presidential campaign, Ralph Nader stopped in for a cuppa. A photo of him sitting at his table showed up on The Tonight Show. Jay Leno quipped, "And here is Ralph Nader sitting with all his friends at The Grounds Keeper in Racine, Wisconsin."

# THE GROUNDS KEEPER

"One need only compare the violent coffee-drinking societies of the West to the peace-loving tea drinker of the Orient to realize the pernicious and malignant effect that bitter brew has upon the human soul."

—Hindu Dietary Tract (author unknown)

Racine
# WILSON'S COFFEE & TEA
3306 Washington Avenue

Wilson's Coffee and Tea opened in October of 1991.

It is a family operation owned by Robin and Diane Wilson.

This is quite a "coffee family".

Their daughter Renae is "generally in charge of everything" at the shop. Son Neal is the shop's coffee roaster and a very good roaster at that.

Last winter, Neal was invited to travel to Addis Ababa, Ethiopia, to partake in an international cupping panel.

That's pretty lofty credentials for a coffee roaster from Wisconsin.

But that international reputation and flair fit the dedication and philosophy of the Wilsons.

They are very good at what they do.

Their goal in opening the shop was to provide the finest whole bean coffee and loose tea to the local community. To reach that goal they spent a year studying the business and researching coffee. All four of the Wilsons traveled to coffee farms and mills in Latin America and Africa, and maintain personal relationships with the growers of their coffee beans.

Robin Wilson summed up the family's business philosophy simply:

"We are the only local coffee roaster, the oldest specialty coffee shop in town, and the only shop in operation for more than a few years that has not been sold once or twice. We seek to provide the finest products in a comfortable, unpretentious environment."

## The Top Ten signs that you may be **DRINKING TOO MUCH COFFEE**

10. When asked who invented the airplane flown at Kitty Hawk, you blurt out "the Hills Brothers".

9. You wonder aloud why hummingbirds are so slow and lethargic.

8. You don't like instant coffee because "it takes too long".

7. You win a Nobel Prize for formulating a new math formula—then quickly forget what you discovered and why you're getting an award.

6. You grind your coffee beans in your mouth.

5. Your teeth begin to resemble your favorite colors: brown and yellow.

4. You get bored watching the Kentucky Derby, complaining that "the race takes too long".

3. All the clouds in the sky are shaped like coffee beans.

2. Your friends record your phone messages and then play them back in slow motion in order to understand you.

1. Juan Valdez names his new donkey after you.

Baa-a-a-ad jokes.

Rice Lake
# NORSKE NOOK OF RICE LAKE
2900 Pioneer Avenue

How good is this place?

Listen to the coffee talk of a group of ladies who meet and drink coffee here six mornings a week.

### The "Toast Ladies of Rice Lake"

"We are a group of grandmother-age ladies who meet six mornings a week to discuss everything, to laugh, to share sorrows, to celebrate birthdays with insulting cards, and to order anything from coffee and toast to the national award-winning pie."

—Gay Christianson

"Great day in the morning, especially if you're at the Norske Nook.

"Daily we friends meet and share much talk and laughter and maybe a problem. We are there for each other."

—Irene Christianson

"We share many laughs, tears, good times and bad times. This time over coffee and good food is better and cheaper than therapy sessions."
—Sue Arnevik

"I lost my dad, mom, and husband within six months. I was reeling when I was invited to morning coffee at the Norske Nook. The coffee, concern, and conversation are just great."
—Sandie Anderson

"There is so much laughter, love, and an abundance of coffee."
—Maridale Jacobson

Rochester
# STIR CRAZY
207 West Main Street

In my mind, this little place represents the real spirit of coffeehouses in Wisconsin.

It is in one of the smallest towns that I found on my journey. In fact, the town is just a few shops, surrounded by a cluster of charming, century-old homes.

Its claim to fame is the fact that J. I. Case invented his famous tractor in the same block where Stir Crazy coffee shop is located.

But back to the spirit that I found in these shops.

There is a common denominator that I stumbled upon. It is the fact that size of town has little to do with the success of these places.

Rochester, this tiny burg of humanity, has this coffee shop that has wonderful coffee, delicious baked goods, and tremendous soup that tastes as good as any that I've had in the big cities.

The spirit that I speak of radiates loyalty, enthusiasm, and genuine friendliness. Nothing phony or artificial in the greeting of the owners and fellow customers.

You honestly feel welcomed at this place.

And that warmth I experienced makes me realize that it's not the size of the shop or town, rather, it is the monumental scale of heart and soul that is found in ample abundance at this tiny spot on the map.

Stir crazy?

More like Amazing Graces found in Small Places.

Spring Green
# GENERAL STORE & CAFÉ
137 South Albany Street

Just south of this river town is a lush emerald green valley, known locally as Jones Valley.

It is here, over a century ago, that one of the Jones boys grew up loving nature and its romantic possibilities to combine and harmonize with human dwellings.

The young boy was Frank Lloyd Wright. This was his habitat.

This was his young world. This was his life.

As his reputation grew, this small town became a focal point for global recognition as Wright's hometown. The valley and hollows are filled with examples of his far-reaching architecture. Definitely worth a visit.

Nowadays, the great architect is long gone. But the town has become a haven for creative people.  Architects, Shakespearean actors, musicians, poets, writers, and artists.

The best place for this creative pool to congregate is the General Store.

An old lumberyard building that was converted years ago into a café, coffeehouse, and gift shop.

It is a lively place, the local watering hole featuring such notable events as the annual Bob Fest, held every May when singers come from far and wide to sing back-to-back Bob Dylan songs in tribute to the great midwestern troubadour.

So, if you like your coffee steeped with history and legend this is the place to head on a Sunday morning to sip and savor time.

Stevens Point
# THE SUPREME BEAN
1100 Main Street

"Supreme Bean first opened its doors in November 1989.

"The coffee shop is located midway down Main Street.

"In those early days the little shop primarily served gourmet drip coffee with an occasional order for cappuccino or latte.

"Consumers quickly adapted their palates to the rich, robust flavor of espresso.

"Today most customers order espresso-based drinks ranging from the unadulterated espresso to an iced caramel, or mocha latte.

"The Supreme Bean stocks over 30 varieties of coffee beans on a daily basis."

—Joyce Hamilton, owner


Coffee tip from the author:

Try their Bananas Foster coffee—it was one of the best-flavored coffees that I tasted during my journey.

"The coffee was boiling over a charcoal fire, and large slices of bread and butter were piled one upon the other like deals in a lumber yard."

—Charles Dickens

# STOUGHTON COFFEE BREAK

Hey! Who would have guessed that both the hamburger sandwich and the coffee break were invented in WISCONSIN?

Indeed, the little town of Seymour's alleged claim to fame is that the hamburger sandwich was invented at the Outagamie County Fair in 1885 by a fifteen-year-old named Charlie Nagreen.

And it is well documented that the coffee break was invented in 1871 in Stoughton.

Hey! Who knew?

Back in 1871, tobacco and wagon building were the two main industries in Stoughton and vicinity. Smokes and spokes were the stock and trade of this Norwegian community just south of Madison.

Mr. Osmand Gunderson was seeking men to work in his tobacco warehouse.

He quickly found that all the able-bodied men were hiring on at the local wagon factory.

In despair, Gunderson came up with a brainstorm. Why not ask the local women to work for him sorting and handling tobacco at the warehouse?

The women met with each other and decided they would work for Gunderson with one condition: they would sign on IF he would allow them to return to their homes during the day to have a cup of coffee, check on the children, and prepare the evening meals for their families.

Mr. Gunderson reluctantly agreed, since he needed all the help he could get.

The women signed up and a new milestone was added to world culture—the ritual and habit of a daily coffee break, a brief time to relax and enjoy coffee before heading back to work.

For the past dozen years or so, Stoughton celebrates that landmark moment by holding an annual festival aptly called the Coffee Break Festival.

"Way too much coffee. But, if it weren't for the coffee,
I'd have no identifiable personality whatsoever."

— David Letterman

"Serving coffee on aircraft causes turbulence."

— Author unknown

# Around the Rim and into Iowa
McGregor

# McGREGOR COFFEE ROASTERS

258 Main Street

What makes the perfect roast?

"The perfect coffee roast can be compared to the perfect rib eye steak.

"What is perfect? Could it be rare, medium, well done, or slightly charred?

"They're all actually perfect depending on the taste of the person eating the steak.

"Likewise in roasting coffee.

"The perfect roast is the taste preference of the one cupping the coffee.

"A lighter roast will give more of the flavor of the bean's origin.

"A darker roasted coffee will yield more of a roast flavor.

"The importance of roasting:

"In the early twentieth century, Americans were turned on by mass produced canned and processed foods.

"We didn't have to worry about growing fresh vegetables, and raising our own livestock for meat. At the time, we thought this was wonderful.

"In the twenty-first century, we now realize the huge benefits of eating fresh, and our modern taste buds appreciate much higher quality food and beverages.

"Fresh food co-ops are popping up everywhere around the country.

"We have seen the passion wine lovers have for the finest quality of wines.

"For the beer lovers, we have seen the proliferation of microbreweries nationwide.

"But unfortunately, for most of America's coffee drinkers, the norm is still canned, tasteless, and bland stale coffee from the store shelf.

"I believe that we coffee lovers are on the verge of our own 'coffee revolution' moving forward to a day when 'Fresh Roasted on Site' will be the norm rather than the extreme".

—Ted, head roaster, McGregor Coffee Roasters

McGregor, Iowa

# THE TWISTED CHICKEN

212 Main Street

Owner Kim Hays relates the tale:

"In 1988, we moved to Prairie du Chien and purchased a very picturesque but very dysfunctional and defunct farm.

"Among the rundown outbuildings was a chicken coop.

"We decided that we would get a bunch of laying hens and have fresh eggs. We looked in a Murray McMurray hatchery catalog and picked out fifty assorted hens to be shipped to the farm. They arrived as day-old chicks and we proceeded to raise them by the book.

"When the hens were two weeks old, we noticed that six or seven of them had dowager's humps and were bent and twisted. Some even walked sideways.

**92**

"We questioned 'by the book' methods wondering what we might be doing wrong to have caused this physical aberration.

"After a thorough orthopedic exam we decided nothing was broken and we declared them healthy, but twisted.

"The hens proceeded to live normal lives, clustering together, seemingly to know that they were special … someday to be famous.

"As a group they roamed freely through the farmyard, eating, sunning and dust bathing.

"One day we decided to call them 'the twisted chickens'.

"The name stuck.

"Eventually they all passed on to roam that 'big free-range farmyard in the sky' leaving us only fond memories.

"They all lived a normal five to six years on planet Wisconsin.

"Years later, when it came time to pick a name for the restaurant, we recalled 'Twisted Chickens' and decided that this eatery would be named after the last of the twisted chickens and their legacy."

# Around the Rim and into Minnesota

## Duluth

# BEANERS CENTRAL

324 North Central Avenue

On the western edge of Duluth, this place is a coffeehouse centered on both the musical and visual arts.

In its own way it is an artist's clubhouse offering coffee lovers up to 200 different musical acts each year and a new visual artist exhibiting every month.

Beaners offers music five to seven nights per week with up to four different acts per night. This place is so musically oriented that many of the staff members play in the bands that perform.

Beaners has its own CD of musical groups that have appeared on stage here over the years.

Owner Jason Wussow started the coffeehouse eight years ago and built it around the arts.

Jason is planning to build a recording studio downstairs to further the musical legacy of this little music box on Central Avenue.

Not only does it offer great music, coffee, and sandwiches but the visual arts are represented as well.

Certainly the most unusual artwork displayed here was a show of paintings by two Duluth artists, Angel and Andy Sarkela-Sauer.

Angel and Andy created a new, yet old, medium for their show.

They paint with Coffee!

(Yes, I said Coffee.)

Angel and Andy mix coffee with other media to create beautiful sepia tinted watercolors.

Does it work as an art medium?

Well, their first show sold out. They have since painted over 200 coffee paintings and they are selling like ... well, like hot coffee on a cold Minnesota morning.

Minneapolis

# COLUMBIA GROUNDS

3301 Central Avenue N. E.

This is a nice little coffeehouse in northeast Minneapolis which provides an atmosphere as rich and robust as a good cup of steaming java.

Several nights a week there is live music played at the shop that varies from polka bands to bluegrass to vintage rock and roll.

A section of Columbia Grounds is devoted to the work of local artists.

Perhaps the biggest feature is the outdoor garden and patio behind the store, a great place to sip coffee and take in the music and soft breezes of a spring morning in Minnesota.

•

"Everybody should believe in something.
I believe I'll have another cup of coffee."

—Author unknown

Garden of Earthly Delights

Uptown District of Minneapolis
# ISLES BUN & COFFEE
1424 West 28th Street

Opening the screen door here at Isles ushers a stranger into a delightful world of heavenly scents and home-baked fragrance.

The sweet scent of bakery goods and fresh coffee brewing lingers in the air.

As I ponder the showcase of baked "goodies" I spy a long bun that looks like a glazed donut that has gone straight.

I ask the counter man, "What's that?"

"Puppy dog tail," he replies.

I think, oh what the hell, try something new, so I order one.

I realize that for most of my life, I have always picked out bakery delights that have more than ample amounts of frosting upon them.

I confess "frosting is my thing" ever since my mom used to let me lick the spoon back in cookie-making days of youth.

"You like frosting?" the counter man asks.

"Oh yeah, I'm addicted."

"Well, you've come to the right place. Turn around and look at the cream and sugar counter."

ISLES
BUN & COFFEE

Smack dab in the middle of the coffee "fixings" is a large silver bowl with a big spatula sticking out of its center.

"Frosting, help yourself!" he exclaims.

As I load up and eat my puppy dog tail and sip my coffee, I realize, indeed this is heaven on earth.

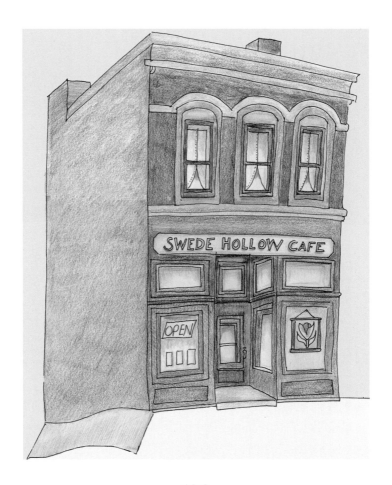

St. Paul
# ſWEDE HOLLOW CAFÉ
725 East Seventh Street

This little curbside café is perched high above an old neighborhood of St. Paul that for years was the home to immigrant workers of Swedish, Italian, and Mexican origins.

The neighborhood was a collection of small buildings built around Phalen Creek.

It had its own lineage and character, providing housing for unskilled and semiskilled workers who arrived here by train. The little village in a hollow was close enough to downtown St. Paul that the residents could walk to work.

Back then, this little shop on Seventh Street was a cigar shop.

Nowadays the shop doesn't emit any cigar smoke; rather, the aromatic scent of coffee and homemade soup wafts out the door.

The most unusual feature offered here is the view.

One can take a cup of coffee and plate of food out on a terraced side yard that overlooks both the tiny hollow below and the towering skyline of St. Paul.

A room with a view.

St. Paul
# COFFEE NEWS CAFÉ
1662 Grand Avenue


When I travel to large cities, I actively seek out those "little towns within the city" neighborhoods.

You know the kind—those little crossroad business communities that harken back to the days when an ethnic group started an inner city business settlement that stretched along the streetcar tracks.

Places that ooze with unique shops and one-of-a-kind merchants.

Places that are still alive with character.

Whenever I travel to St. Paul, Grand Avenue is one of my first stops, particularly the neighborhood around Macalester College. It has an interesting collection of art shops, ethnic eateries, and one unique coffee shop, Coffee News Café.

Years ago, I used to migrate here for a wonderful bookstore that was on the end of the block. It was called The Hungry Mind and had a great café inside cleverly titled Table of Contents.

But it closed a few years ago, causing me to wander down the street a few doors to this classic coffee shop—Coffee News Café.

It has become my new neighborhood stop.

"Don't roast your coffee beans in the marketplace."
(Don't tell secrets to strangers.)

— Ancient Oromo Nomad saying

# Where the Coffeehouses are in Wisconsin...

ASHLAND
The Black Cat
211 Chapple Ave.
Ashland, WI 54806
715-682-3680

BAYFIELD
Burt & Francie's Café
117 Rittenhouse Ave.
Bayfield, WI 54814
715-779-9619

BURLINGTON
The Daily Brew
557 Milwaukee Ave.
Burlington, WI 53105
262-767-9951

CORNUCOPIA
Siskiwit Bay Coffee
& Curiosities
88610 Superior Ave.
Cornucopia, WI 54827
715-742-3388

DE PERE
Luna Coffee Roasters
330 Main Ave.
De Pere, WI 54115
920-336-1557

EAGLE RIVER
Terra Nicole's
711 D Hwy. 45 North
Eagle River, WI 54521
715-479-8215

EPHRAIM
Leroy's Coffee
9922 Water St.
Ephraim, WI 54211
920-854-4044

EVANSVILLE
Real Coffee
18 E. Main St.
Evansville, WI 53536
608-882-0949

HAYWARD
Backroads Coffee & Tea
10546 Dakota Ave.
Hayward, WI 54843
715-634-4950

HURLEY
Hurley Coffee Company
122 Silver St.
Hurley, WI 54534
715-561-5500

KENOSHA
Common Grounds
5159 Sixth Ave.
Kenosha, WI 53140
262-652-5111

LA CROSSE
Jules' Coffee House
327 Pearl St.
La Crosse, WI 54601
608-796-1200

MADISON

Cargo Coffee
1309 S. Park St.
Madison, WI 53715
608-220-7910

Fair Trade Coffeehouse
418 State St.
Madison, WI 53703
608-268-0477

Lazy Jane's Café
1358 Williamson St.
Madison, WI 53703
608-257-5263

Michelangelo's Coffee House
114 State St.
Madison, WI 53703
608-251-5299

Steep & Brew
544 State St.
Madison, WI 53703
608-256-2902

MENOMONIE

Legacy Chocolates
643 S. Broadway Ave.
Menomonie, WI 54751
715-231-2580

MILWAUKEE

Alterra Coffee Roasters
1701 N. Lincoln Memorial Dr.
Milwaukee, WI 53202
414-223-4551

Rochambo Coffee & Tea
1317 E. Brady St.
Milwaukee, WI 53202
414-291-0095

MOUNT HOREB

Sjölinds Chocolate House
219 E. Main St.
Mt. Horeb, WI 53572
608-437-0233

PLATTEVILLE

Badger Brothers Coffee
10 E. Main St.
Platteville, WI 53818
608-348-7764

PRAIRIE DU SAC

Blue Spoon Café
550 Water St.
Prairie du Sac, WI 53578
608-643-0837

RACINE

The Grounds Keeper
327 Main St.
Racine, WI 53403
262-638-8336

Milaeger's Java Garden Café
4838 Douglas Ave.
Racine, WI 53402
262-639-2040

Mocha Lisa
2825 4 ½ Mile Rd.
Racine, WI 53402
262-681-2644

Wilson's Coffee & Tea
3306 Washington Ave.
Racine, WI 53405
262-634-6611

# …And Beyond the Rim

RICE LAKE
Norske Nook
of Rice Lake
2900 Pioneer Ave.
Rice Lake, WI 54868
715-234-1733

ROCHESTER
Stir Crazy
207 W. Main St.
Rochester, WI 53167
262-534-1929

SPRING GREEN
General Store & Café
137 S. Albany St.
Spring Green, WI 53588
608-588-7070

STEVENS POINT
The Supreme Bean
1100 Main St.
Stevens Point, WI 54481
715-344-0077

McGREGOR, IOWA
McGregor Coffee Roasters
258 Main St.
McGregor, IA 52157

The Twisted Chicken
212 Main St.
McGregor, IA 52157
563-873-1515

DULUTH, MINNESOTA
Beaners Central
324 N. Central Ave.
Duluth, MN 55807
218-624-5957

MINNEAPOLIS, MINNESOTA
Columbia Grounds
3301 Central Ave. N.E.
Minneapolis, MN 55418
612-781-7873

Isles Bun & Coffee
1424 W. 28th St.
Minneapolis, MN 55408
612-870-4466

ST. PAUL, MINNESOTA
Coffee News Café
1662 Grand Ave.
St. Paul, MN 55105
651-698-3324

Swede Hollow Café
725 E. Seventh St.
St. Paul, MN 55106
651-776-8810

# CODA

I found a wonderful cozy log cabin for the night perched just upriver from The Twisted Chicken.

The cabin offered a nice perspective of the lights of Wisconsin glimmering across the Mississippi River from me. It also offered a nice inner perspective of this whole three-year journey.

What did I find on this java odyssey? What did I learn about coffeehouses in Wisconsin? Well, I learned more about humanity than about "the perfect brew".

I ventured out to over 100 coffee shops thinking that these places would have interesting possibilities for interviews (like my fish fry and hamburger books) and perhaps a twist on the new culture of a good cup of coffee in the Heartland.

Shortly into the journey, I realized that coffee is just the tip of the iceberg.

There is a depth of human character here that is as deep as a bottomless cup of coffee.

I found that these places have exceptional coffee, but there is something much deeper residing in these little Dairyland establishments.

These places have become community centers.

Pat and Kris Clark, who own and operate the Daily Brew in Burlington, touched on this in an e-mail that they sent me. "We moved to Burlington from Michigan five years ago. We worried about how we would be accepted as outsiders in a new town. As it turned out, our fears were unfounded. We were accepted with open arms. The town soon adopted our coffee shop as a meeting place, a clubhouse, a gallery, a place to drop off things, and the unofficial box office of the town.

"Besides the usual meeting over coffee and food, people routinely drop things off for their friends to pick up later. We had our local Cornwall Tool driver drop off a power saw for a client to pick up. An entire real estate deal between several people took place at the Brew. We also have developed into a box office. This started with the community theatre, now it has morphed into a ticket exchange that ranges from pancake breakfasts to garden walks.

"And then there is the newsletter, which we started just to let people know what our soup specials would be for the week. One of our customers asked us if we could mention an event and now the newsletter includes a potpourri of community events including theatre, garden walks, music concerts, rummage sales, spaghetti dinners and a 'thought for the weekly.'"


I wonder: what have I learned from this journey?

I've learned that these little places serve more then coffee and scones. They

111

provide old-fashioned values of genuine conversation, bottomless vessels of humor, and unpretentious concern for our neighbors.

I've learned that they are support systems, comfort zones, and trustworthy refuges to migrate to during times when one's heart is low and lonely.

I've learned that many people seek them out as a safe place between home and work.

I've learned that they are sacred places for the soul, a quiet place to rest from the storms of humanity.

I've learned that in many small towns, they are the center of the universe to meet, to congregate, to laugh, and to cry. They are anchors of comfort and support.

A coffee drinker in Stoughton put it to me in simple words:

"Jeff, this is not a coffee house, this is a coffee HOME."

People who share a deep kinship for others—their common denominator is a strong loyalty for one particular small coffee shop on Main Street. Profound places for the soul tucked away in Dairyland. Thank goodness for their existence!

Yes, there is an awakening here. I went out to sip coffee in small towns and cities in Wisconsin.

The unexpected reward I encountered was the sugar of life that I found in each one of these places which made the experience a whole lot sweeter than I ever imagined.